HIGH VOICE

WITH A CD OF PIANO
ACCOMPANIMENTS

15 ART SONGS BY AMERICAN COMPOSERS

SONGS BY
ARGENTO, BERNSTEIN, CHANLER,
COPLAND, DUKE, HUNDLEY,
AND ROREM

BOOSEY & HAWKES

AN **IMAGEM** COMPANY

DISTRIBUTED BY

HAL•LEONARD®
CORPORATION
7777 W. BLUEMOUND RD. P.O. BOX 13819 MILWAUKEE, WI 53213

www.boosey.com
www.halleonard.com

CONTENTS

Pianist on the CD: Laura Ward

for Nicholas Di Virgilio

Winter

from *Six Elizabethan Songs*

original key

WILLIAM SHAKESPEARE

DOMINICK ARGENTO

In accompaniment recording, the first vocal note is played three times before the entrance.

for Nicholas Di Virgilio
Spring
from *Six Elizabethan Songs*
original key

THOMAS NASH

DOMINICK ARGENTO

Spring is like a perhaps hand

from *Songs about Spring*

original key

e.e. cummings

DOMINICK ARGENTO

Jupiter has seven moons

from *I Hate Music!*
original key

Words and Music by
LEONARD BERNSTEIN

I hate music!

from *I Hate Music!*

original key

Words and Music by
LEONARD BERNSTEIN

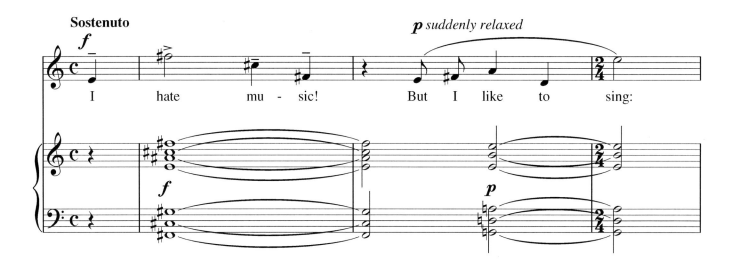

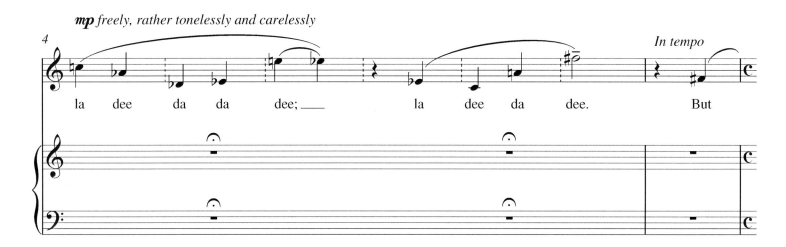

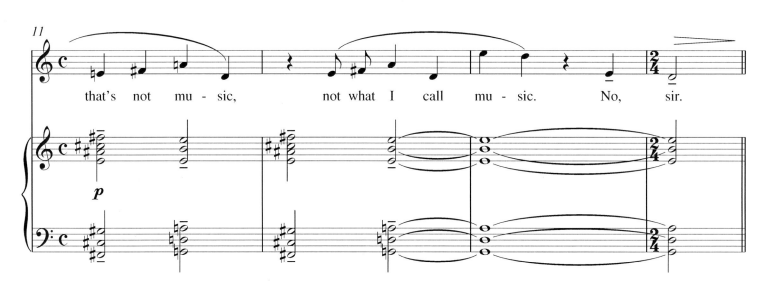

In accompaniment recording, the first vocal note is played three times before the entrance.

These, My Ophelia

original key

ARCHIBALD MACLEISH

THEODORE CHANLER

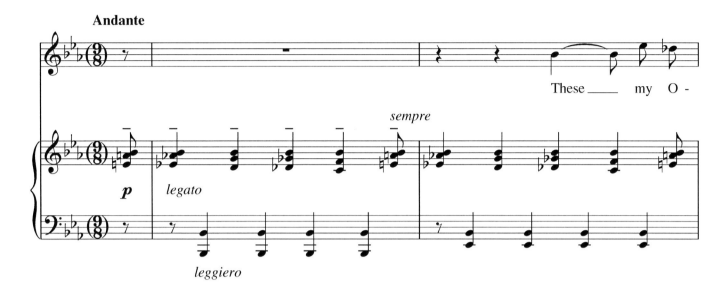

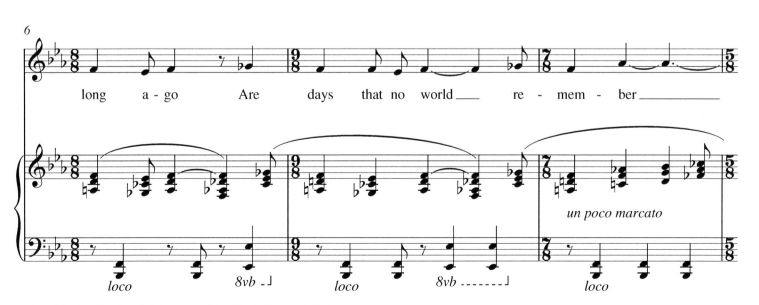

And our yes-ter-day ___ O ___ my O-phel - ia ___

___ Shall be the eve-ning star   For some

earth that turns ___ from Arc-tur - us   When we no long-er my O-phel - ia

Come here to the oak a - bove the sea ___

Ching-a-ring Chaw
(Minstrel Song)

from *Old American Songs, Set II*

original key: D Major

Arranged by
AARON COPLAND

To Ingolf Dahl

Why do they shut me out of Heaven?

from *Twelve Poems of Emily Dickinson*

original key

EMILY DICKINSON

AARON COPLAND

trou-bled them _____ But don't shut the door, don't _____ shut the door. _____

Somewhat faster (♩ = 88)

Oh if I were the gen-tle-men in the

white robes and they were the lit-tle hand that knocked, _____

To Marcelle de Manziarly

Heart, we will forget him

from *Twelve Poems of Emily Dickinson*

original key

EMILY DICKINSON

AARON COPLAND

* Grace note on the beat

To the memory of my grandmother

The Astronomers
(An Epitaph)
original key

RICHARD HUNDLEY

Based on an inscription
found in Allegheny, Pa.

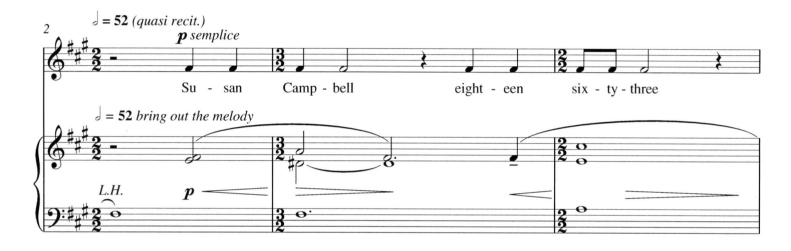

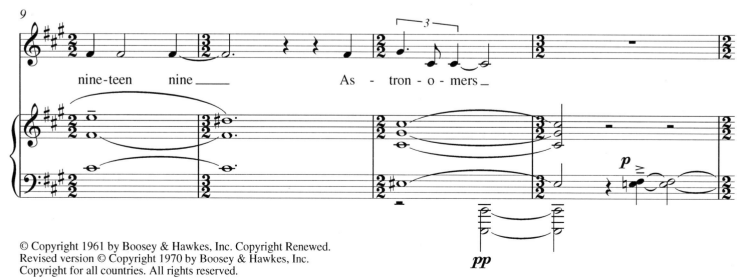

Sept. 1959, New York City

Jeanie with the Light Brown Hair

original key: a whole step lower

STEPHEN FOSTER
arranged by
NED ROREM

Sigh - ing like the night wind and sob - bing like the rain,

Wail - ing for the lost one that comes not a - gain: I

long for Jean-ie and my heart bows _ low,

Nev-er more to find her where the

bright wa - ters flow. _____

Nantucket, 22–23 May 1982

O Do Not Love Too Long

original key: a whole step lower

WILLIAM BUTLER YEATS

NED ROREM

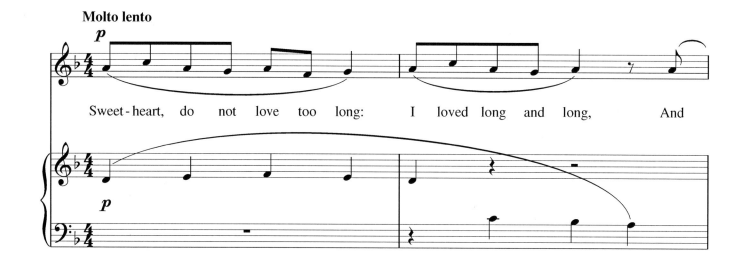

In accompaniment recording, the first vocal/piano notes are played before the entrance.

Marrakech, 20 April 1951

To Julien Green

What if some little pain...
original key

EDMUND SPENSER

NED ROREM

Fez, Morocco, 20 December 1949
(14:30)

Central Park at Dusk
original key

SARA TEASDALE*

JOHN DUKE

*From "Collected Poems" by Sara Teasdale (Macmillan)

There is no sign of leaf or bud A hush is o-ver

eve-ry-thing. Si - lent as wom-en wait for love

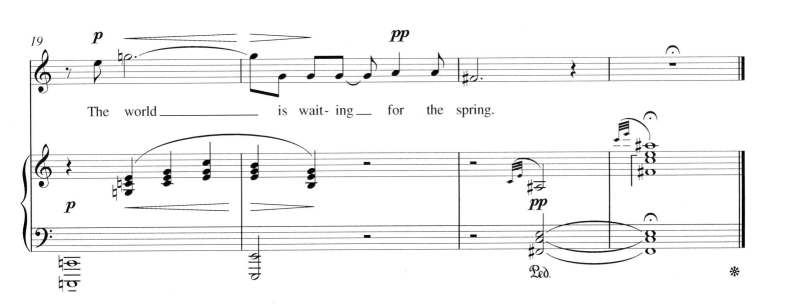

The world is wait-ing for the spring.

There will be stars
original key

SARA TEASDALE*

JOHN DUKE

*From "Collected Poems" by Sara Teasdale (Macmillan)

Still - ness will be deep;

There will be stars _____ o - ver the place for - ev - er,

There will be stars _____ for -

ev - er, while we sleep. _____